Crossing Guards

By JoAnn Early Macken

Gareth Stevens
Publishing

Please visit our Web site, www.garethstevens.com. For a free color catalog of all our high-quality books, call toll free 1-800-542-2595 or fax 1-877-542-2596.

Library of Congress Cataloging-in-Publication Data

Macken, JoAnn Early, 1953-
Crossing guards / JoAnn Early Macken.
    p. cm. – (People in my community)
Includes index.
ISBN 978-1-4339-3798-9 (pbk.)
ISBN 978-1-4339-3799-6 (6-pack)
ISBN 978-1-4339-3797-2 (library binding)
1. School crossing guards. I. Title.
LB2865.M332 2011
363.12'57–dc22
                        2010013963

New edition published 2011 by
Gareth Stevens Publishing
111 East 14th Street, Suite 349
New York, NY 10003

New text and images this edition copyright © 2011 Gareth Stevens Publishing

Original edition published 2003 by Weekly Reader® Books
An imprint of Gareth Stevens Publishing
Original edition text and images copyright © 2003 Gareth Stevens Publishing

Art direction: Haley Harasymiw, Tammy Gruenwald
Page layout: Daniel Hosek, Katherine A. Goedheer
Editorial direction: Kerri O'Donnell, Diane Laska Swanke

Photo credits: Cover, back cover, p. 1 Andersen Ross/Getty Images; pp. 5, 9, 11, 15, 19 © Gregg Andersen; p. 7 Shutterstock.com; p. 13 David Buffington/Getty Images; p. 17 © iStockphoto.com; p. 21 Shawn Thew/ AFP/Getty Images.

Printed in the United States of America

CPSIA compliance information: Batch #CS10GS: For further information contact Gareth Stevens, New York, New York at 1-800-542-2595.

Table of Contents

Boldface words appear in the glossary.

An Important Job

A crossing guard helps children walk to school safely. A crossing guard stops **traffic** so that children can cross the street.

A crossing guard may hold up a stop sign or a **flag**. Stop signs and flags tell drivers to stop.

stop sign

Drivers watch the crossing guard. They stop when the guard says to. Then children can safely cross the street.

Children wait on the **corner**. The crossing guard tells them when it is safe for them to cross the street.

Sometimes, a crossing guard walks with the children as they cross the street. This helps to keep them safe.

Safety First!

Crossing guards know important safety rules. They know how to tell drivers when to stop and when to go.

Crossing guards wear bright **vests** or coats. The bright color helps drivers see them.

Do you know how to safely cross a street? Always wait at a corner. Be sure to stay on the sidewalk. Look both ways before you cross!

Never run into the street. Listen to the crossing guard. This will keep you safe!

Glossary

corner: the place where two streets meet

flag: a piece of cloth used as a symbol

traffic: cars, trucks, buses, and other things moving on the street

vest: a short, sleeveless jacket

For More Information

Books

Humphreys, Paul. *Look Out on the Road*. London, UK: Evans Brothers Ltd., 2003.

Rivera, Sheila. *Crossing Safety*. Minneapolis, MN: Lerner Publishing Group, 2007.

Web Sites

Safe Walking for Kids
www.safeny.com/Kids/kidswalk.htm
This site shows common traffic signs and teaches the safe way to cross the street.

Traffic Sign Quiz for Kids
www.safeny.com/Kids/kidssign.htm
A fun site using traffic signs. See if you know what they mean.

Index

About the Author

JoAnn Early Macken is the author of children's poetry; two rhyming picture books, *Cats on Judy* and *Sing-Along Songs*; and various other nonfiction series. She teaches children to write poetry and received the Barbara Juster Esbensen 2000 Poetry Teaching Award. JoAnn is a graduate of the MFA in Writing for Children Program at Vermont College. She lives in Wisconsin with her husband and their two sons.